MEXICO
Houses of the Pacific

MEXICO
Houses of the Pacific

MARIE-PIERRE COLLE
Text & Production

PEDRO RAMIREZ VAZQUEZ
IIntroduction

IGNACIO URQUIZA
Photography

XAVIER PIZARRO
Design

ALTI
PUBLISHING

MEXICO:
Houses of the Pacific

ALTI Publishing would like to express gratitude to Mr. Manuel Arango for having suggested the concept of this book. Without his on-going, enthusiastic and generous support, it would not exist.

ALTI Publishing
4180 La Jolla Village Drive, Suite 520
La Jolla, California 92037 Phone: (619) 452-7703

MARIE-PIERRE COLLE: Text and Production
PEDRO RAMIREZ VAZQUEZ: Introduction
IGNACIO URQUIZA: Photography
JAVIER PIZARRO: Design
GABRIEL LOERA: Editorial Consultant
ADELA SALINAS: Copy Editor
RENE LOPEZ: Assistant Photographer
RICHARD LINDLEY: Translation

Published in the United States of America.

Library of Congress Catalog Card Number 94-071534
ISBN 1-883051-02-9

Photographs on cover and page 82: Fundación Mexicana para la Educación Ambiental A.C. / M. Calderwood
Photographs on pages 196–199: Lourdes Legorreta.
Printed in Japan by Toppan Printing Company

Our special thanks to architect Pedro Ramírez Vázquez for enriching this book with his introduction.

I am most grateful for the hospitality and generosity of Enrique Aldrete, Marie-Thérèse and Manuel Arango, Gianfranco Brignone, Nicole Dugal, Meche and Manuel Felguérez, Heather and Carlos Herrera, Tony Murray, Norma and Rodolfo Ogarrio, Willy Urrea, Malena and José de Yturbe, Hotel Zaashila in Huatulco, as well as Yvonne and Jacques Baldassari, Eduardo González Padilla, Laura and Eduardo Legorreta, Mónica and Carlos Silva, Delfina Vargas, Tita and Manuel Vizcaíno, and numerous other anonymous friends.

Thanks also to the owners of the houses that unfortunately could not be included in this publication. Architects Marco Aldaco, Mario Lazo, Ricardo Legorreta, Manolo Mestre and Diego Villaseñor offered many valuable suggestions. Dear Tere Castelló contributed the hammock story. To my agent Bárbara Hogenson, my thanks for her work on our second book. As always, Eric Giebeler, my son, is present on this journey. Guillermo Grimm, that great connoisseur of the Pacific Coast, warmly supported the project.

I owe a vote of thanks to Francisco Arce, Elisa Castellano van Rhijn, Juana Cruz, Viviana Dean, María del Carmen Elizalde, Aurora García, René López, Gustavo Martínez, Sandra O'Rourke, Rosalba Ramírez, Guadalupe Rosales, Anita de Seoane, Lorenza Trejo Lerdo, Juan José Silva, Stacey Symonds, Yvonne Tron, Alicia Trueba, Nidia Veltheer, Max Zamora and my assistant Adriana Auza, who worked so diligently.

Gabriel Loera, faithful friend, assisted greatly in developing the concept of the book. Robert Amram, Tonatiuh Gutiérrez and José Manuel Muradás all provided excellent critiques.

Adela Salinas improved the text with great editorial sensitivity. Javier Pizarro achieved a unique rhythm in the design of the book and provided worthy settings for Ignacio Urquiza's extraordinary photographs.

To ALTI Publishing and its President, Wayne B. Hilbig, thanks for having made this book a reality.

My thanks to this outstanding team.

Marie-Pierre Colle

CONTENTS

PROLOGUE

As architect Luis Barragán used to say, the real façade of a house is the sky, and an authentic architecture is one that conveys a message of beauty and emotion.

This book is an invitation to feel the sense of Mexican architecture along the 2,000 miles of Pacific coastline of the states of Baja California, Nayarit, Jalisco, Colima, Guerrero and Oaxaca. This is an architecture of light and shadow, of fragrances, water and sand.

The Pacific Coast, with its prodigal natural settings rich in sources of inspiration and fantasy, has always held a special attraction for Mexican architects like Marco Aldaco, Santiago Aspe, Jean Dwlit, Carlos Herrera, Guillermo Hume, Ricardo Legorreta, Manolo Mestre, Enrique Müller, Ignacio Rodríguez, Javier Sordo, Diego Villaseñor, Manuel Vizcaíno, Guillermo Wulff, José de Yturbe and Enrique Zozaya, who have worked to incorporate their creations into the sensual beauty of the coast. They have renounced the international style. Local ecology and indigenous cultural roots are for them a respected, even exalted, source of inspiration. They have opened the door to simple local pleasures, to tropical aromas, to cross-ventilation. Their interiors echo the outdoors, giving birth to a unique style, to a new philosophy of living.

Attracted by the strength and serenity of the landscape, they have used a free-ranging imagination to rediscover the emblematic form and space of the coastal house. They have created a style rooted in indigenous traditions and cut to modern measure. Native architecture, transfigured in our day, fulfills the dreams of some and becomes the reality of others.

Scanty rainfall and warm days and nights have allowed the palapa, a thatched-roof shelter, to serve as the centerpiece of residential architecture on the coast, where people are free to live without doors or windows.

One of the first contemporary houses in what is called the "new palapa" was designed in 1970 by architect Marco Aldaco at Acapulco, for Loel and Gloria Guinness. Gloria is the muse who inspired this new Mexican style, in which the palapa communicates with nature through a space without glass windows, a space filled with handicraft tailored to the scale of the house.

The living and dining areas are sheltered under the one great roof. Separate bedrooms foster privacy. Rounded walls serve to shield the interior from sunlight and noise. One lives into the elements of space, light and shadow, walls and areas. The house is redolent with the fragrance of ripe fruit, the aroma of the sea. We feel the burning sand, the warm water . . . we become tropical.

Here, where the wind runs under the shade of the palapa, idling among the palm groves, in the clear light of surrender, where one feels the vanishing of an infinite expectancy, where the sun chases all shadows and plunges them into the horizon is where *Mexico: Houses of the Pacific*, was born.

INTRODUCTION

Man lives in the certitude of having his own space and being able to inhabit it. A house is much more than protection against the elements, it is the pillar of man and in it are the limits of his essential space; the interior and the exterior space, of the individual and of the society in which he lives; his longings and his actions. The house reflects one's manner of being, of living, of thinking, and of creating.

The Mexican house is ingeniously built. It sums up ancestral customs and astonishes us with the simplicity of its beauty. The purity of its lines, the authenticity of its materials and the spirit of its form all speak of people and towns who have resolved their living space with wisdom.

In traveling around our country, one can see how each region, each climate, culture and tradition determine the form and materials of our buildings. The Mexican house is a result of—and a lesson in—reason, function, beauty and gravity.

The popular Mexican house is also a product of accumulated experience and of ancient tradition, a tradition often deprecated and rejected by an architecture that boasts of being "modern." This architecture prefers to follow North American models and stereotypes that are foreign not only to our geography and climate, but also to our culture and life needs.

Traditional housing in our country is conditioned by two types of influence, one historical and the other natural. The natural influence is determined by climate and natural resources. The historical influence is comprised of the effects of our cultural traditions, both the pre-Columbian and the Spanish.

Climate determines the need for protection. A house must safeguard its inhabitants from the ferocity of growing vegetation, from rainfall, floods and other natural phenomena. Thus man, through his dwellings, creates microclimates that enhance his existence. Atmospheric conditions form one of the main reasons for building houses, which are spaces created by and for man himself and designed to temper environmental conditions.

Natural resources, on the other hand, determine which materials are at his disposal for building and creating the housing typical of each region. Cultural tradition, for its part, provides the technological means by which materials are exploited and transformed in different types of building systems and procedures. It also determines the ways in which the local inhabitants will deal with climate-related needs and their economic context.

Now more than ever, the influence of new industrial materials and building techniques has penetrated the ambience of the traditional house, creating hybrids that not only fail to meet the needs of their residents, but also, lamentably, transform the traditional image of the house with the use of modern materials.

A singular group of Mexican architects has reevaluated and reinterpreted the traditional use of natural resources and the role of climate in the houses of the Pacific Coast. The result is a dwelling thoroughly integrated into the environment, inviting its residents to enjoy the pleasures of nature as well as human companionship. This new type of house sets aside technological sophistication and architectural fashion in favor of using locally abundant raw materials of proven efficacy, such as adobe, palm, reed, wood and stone.

Mexico: Houses of the Pacific sums up the experiences and achievements of this group of architects. Through these pages, we can verify not only that the architectural models native to the Pacific Coast can be developed and improved with appropriate technology, but also that it is possible to revitalize and recreate these models in an imaginative way.

Along a wide band fronting the Pacific and comprising the states of Baja California Sur, Nayarit, Jalisco, Colima, Guerrero and Oaxaca, this intriguing architecture is developing, and the outstanding fact is that its changes and adaptations do not essentially modify or violate the traditional models, but rather take advantage of and reinterpret them. A daring architecture has been created that is part of an experience accumulated over several centuries. One of its most interesting characteristics is that it achieves an atmosphere of integration and communication with nature. Houses not only come to be a part of the landscape, but in some cases dissolve, merge with, and even come to mimic the landscape. In other cases, the landscape is so artfully framed through window openings that it becomes a part of the house itself.

The rainy tropical climate has long had a determining influence on the architectural solutions common to this region, and this new group of architects has fully adapted to this circumstance. They have sought to orient their houses to the prevailing breezes in order to keep them cooler. In most of this zone the winters are actually rather hot, so doorways have been minimized. When doors do exist, they—like the window openings—are located opposite one another in order to provide for cross-ventilation.

The best roof for this climate is one that allows rainwater to run off rapidly. For this reason, most roofs have either two or more pitches, or else they are conical, with the degree of pitch determined by the type of materials used. Most are covered with palm-leaf thatching or tile, depending on the locale, the architect's preference and the relationship of the house to its surroundings.

These types of roof require wide overhangs in order to protect the walls from rain-induced erosion, as well as to avoid or reduce the incidence of sunlight. Using palm-leaf thatch to cover the roof has a dual effect: on the one hand it serves to integrate the house with its surroundings, and on the other, it attenuates the heat due to its low conductance and the thousands of tiny air pockets created between successive layers of palm-leaf. When clay tile is chosen for the roof covering instead, the same effect is achieved, as an intermediate layer of air provides insulation from the heat.

Among the architectural forms now in use, one that stands out for its beauty and functionality is the round house with a conical roof. It has the added advantage that whatever the wind direction, the house is always adequately ventilated. Also, its walls offer no surfaces perpendicular to the sun's rays, so it absorbs less heat.

One of the most interesting characteristics of this architectural style is its marked preference for smooth transitions in the angles formed by columns and spaces. On can even say that right angles are systematically avoided. The corners formed by walls and columns are also rounded, so that the total effect is extremely sensual to the eye. This is an architecture that takes up and reconfigures the contrast between forms, while at the same time striving for an intentionally smooth transition, thus surprising us with its beauty and originality.

The use of color contributes to emphasizing the play of form against form while enlivening the building. Sometimes color is used cautiously, following the traditional vernacular color palette, while some builders use color with an audaciousness that borders on sophistication. It is color that allows us to appreciate and reaffirm the particularly Mexican taste for contrast, and an ongoing relationship is maintained with the traditional color sensibilities and practices of pre-Hispanic cultures.

The climate and geography of the coast plays a significant role in the selection of color and its luminosity, both of which reveal individual and collective personalities and tastes. Mexicans are accustomed to high contrast, but for foreigners, the color of our houses is even more impressive, due to the play of light and shadow that it provokes.

The simple reeds of ramadas and shutters blending light, shadow and color with effects that resemble physical textures are extremely attractive, while also allowing free air circulation.

The flooring in halls and living spaces is complemented by an admirable combination of pebblestone that, on occasion, reminds one of the designs woven into traditional petates. The interior decoration achieves simplicity and congruence with the infinite variety of furniture, tiles and objects of daily use provided by Mexican handcrafts.

To sum up, *Mexico: Houses of the Pacific* is a book that was needed in our country. It is a valuable book in that it provides young architects with an orientation and leads them to reflect on the rich variety of forms they can achieve if they take as their point of departure a reevaluation of the environment in which they are building, and base their work on solutions with long-standing survival value that can be revitalized with honesty and intelligence.

Pedro Ramírez Vázquez

Architect

ROOTS

On the Pacific Coast, Mexico sings a
song of a vernacular and contemporary
architecture—where the sea is a
childhood memory that calls forth the
passing of a whale, the flight of a
pelican, a fisherman's boat, a dream of
a seaside architecture where the palapa
drenched in saltwater fills up with sand,
plays with its own freedom and
shares it.

The warmth of the tropics, the
sensuousness of the coast, the
lushness of the jungle, all are decisive
factors in the creation of a house.
Together they call out to the architect
to strive for an open and well-
integrated habitat.

Environment, geography and local
building materials work to foster the
creation of similar architectural styles
in remote areas.

In his first letter to Emperor Charles V,
16th-century conquistador Hernán
Cortés mentions settlements consisting
of adobe houses with stuccoed walls
and straw roofs. The chronicler Sahagún
said of the Indians of Michoacán, "Their
houses were pretty, although all of them
were made of straw."

The palapa, which can be round or rectangular, is descended from the *bohío*, the primitive hut of Yucatán. The palapa is a roof covered with grass or of royal palm leaf cut and assembled during the new moon, when the plant's veins are flooded with sap. It is supported by concrete columns or sometimes with trunks of cayaco palm wound with strangler-fig vines. The walls, more than just partitions or structures, seem wind-sculpted shapes. They interact playfully with the roof and form living sculptures, genies that meet the basic needs of the inhabitants yet sidestep the classical concept of a house.

The palapa, with its many acoustic and thermal advantages, is built from such tropical hardwoods as *xolocuauhtl*, *chacalote*, *quebramachete*, ironwood, and ebony. All are dense woods that insure the building's durability provided they are cut properly to prevent vulnerability to pests. These trees follow a lunar cycle in their growth pattern.

They are also felled under the new moon, then stored in a vertical position for sixty days to allow the sap to flow. They are then cured in seawater for thirty days or more to harden the wood.

At times the structure is lashed together with a very tough fiber made from the edges of maguey leaves. The sharp points left after burning the maguey leaves can be used as needles to sew grass fiber into the cane structure. The lashings can also be made of rattan, or of rope or palm fiber.

These building techniques have changed little since pre-Columbian days. In the last thirty years, however, Mexican architects have become more and more interested in vernacular approaches to construction. They compose with new materials using new techniques. They create, and in so doing, they give back to the sea the romantic ideal of the Mexican home—cheerful and natural, unique in the world for its texture, color, and movement, for its walls and open spaces, for the depths and horizons built into it by the hands of Mexican craftsmen.

INTEGRATION

TEXTURE

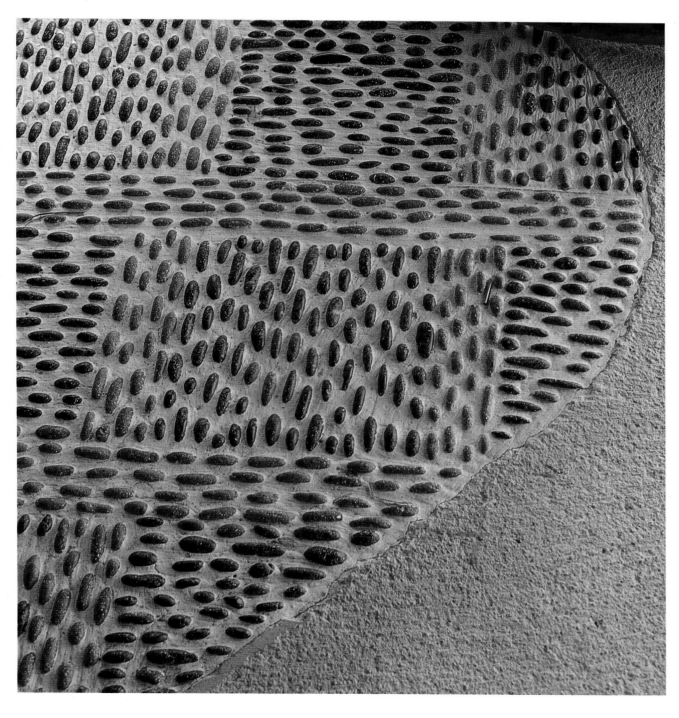

MOVEMENT

PERSPECTIVE

FRAMES

HANDICRAFTS

LOS CABOS

According to legend, California under
the rule of Queen Calafia was an island
of women whose bodies were draped
with gold and pearls. In the course of
his explorations, Cortés arrived there
in 1535 and discovered the place
to be barren and dry—in short,
uninhabitable—and found that it was
not an island but a peninsula.

It was not until the end of the 17th
century that Father Eusebio Kino and
other Jesuit missionaries succeeded in
establishing settlements there.

In its travels from the East, the Manila
Galleon skirted these coasts in search
of pearls. Thus greed came to the land,
and with it those most famous of
pirates—Cromwell, Drake and
Cavendish.

Baja California sand is a warm caress.
The surface of the winter sea is broken
by the long backs of gray whales on
their way to warm southern seas to bear
their young.

In the diaphanous air of Cabo San Lucas among organ pipe cactus, magueys and bishop's weed, architect Jean Dwlit conceived Casa Cazalita, whose arches, columns and clay floors were inspired by the Jesuit missions. Its huge, carved wooden doorway opens out onto the Pacific.

60

PUERTO VALLARTA

The chronicles testify that in 1525 the Aztecs and Toltecs confronted the Spaniards here wielding clubs, darts, bows and arrows, and small banners of colorful feathers—hence the name Bahía de Banderas, the site of modern-day Puerto Vallarta.

After these early revolts, such famous mariners as Sebastián Vizcaíno and the pirate Francis Drake continued periodically to attack this seaport of thatched roofs and palm trees. It was in 1851 that Guadalupe Sánchez and his wife settled the town by moving into the first palapa, where they lived while working to extract gold and silver ore from the deposits of the River Cuale.

In the architectural context of this quaint, semi-tropical seaport, with its narrow streets and hills rolling down toward the sea, this house is typical. Its spacious *redilla* parlors with their tile roofs and brick-and-tile verandas face the church of Our Lady of Guadalupe.

The veranda is the favored area of the house; it faces the setting sun. Flower pots hang from a blue niche. The furniture consists of traditional Jalisco armchairs and tables made of wood and pigskin.

More than 40 years ago, architect Guillermo Wulff arrived in Puerto Vallarta. Using 300-year-old handcrafted building techniques, he left his stamp on local architecture by creating domes in the style of San Miguel de Allende and Guanajuato and using windows with brick lattices manufactured in Jalisco.

Behind the colonial façade of his daughter's house, he conceived a traditional patio where the ornamental tiles, carved Tlaquepaque stone, pebblestone walks, painted flower pots, brick floor and glazed tile fountain recreate a living picture of Andalusia.

Architect Javier Sordo's Casa los Troncos, which graces the Nuevo Vallarta marina, is grand in its conception.

Behind a white façade, imposing yellow pillars sunk in the water along the edge of the corridor lead the visitor past the three pools in one that seem to pour their water directly into the sea.

The entrance gate frames a red sculpture by Sebastián in the middle of the lobby underneath a dome that lets the sunlight pour in.

In the seventh house designed and built by painter Manuel Felguérez and his wife Meche, the living room opens out on Bahía de Banderas. Its wooden European armchairs give the feeling of being on shipboard.

This abstract painter has created a world of beauty to surround him. Next to his bedroom is a study, so he can start painting at the earliest hour.

Casa Pascuarito, on the beach for which it is named, is situated north of Puerto Vallarta and close to Sayulita. The only way to get there is to walk more than half a mile through the jungle.

The cobblestone paths, the mazes rampant with ferns, papelillo trees and chamomile, and the ten conical palapas separated by only a few steps from each other, mingle with the jungle in this harmonious design by architect Miguel Valverde.

Independence is sacred here. Each guest sleeps in an individual palapa next to the sea at Nayarit. And behind the building complex, the jungle with its riot of parakeets, crabs, badgers and *chololos*, shows how the *zalate* is born in palm tree crowns and sends its long roots snaking down their trunks, drawing nourishment from them and twisting them into unusual shapes.

The swimming pool struts its curves, seeming to pour its waters into the Pacific where the fishermen bring their golden carp, their red snapper, octopus, shrimp and lobster.

On the next bay over, architect José de Yturbe has developed a seven-palapa house that echoes the rocky Nayarit landscape.

He felt the land with his heart as well as with his senses. He gathered and saved even the smallest twig and collected the rocks needed to frame the windows.

He conceived every element based on a square inscribed in a circle. He set aside straight lines in favor of curves that adapt to the landscape and proliferate into infinity.

A spacious patio with seventeen cyclopean pillars stretches itself over a paved and terraced floor, stimulating the memory to travel through the Orient, to the rice terraces of China's valleys—only these terraces have rounded pebbles and are bordered by low snaking walls.

A slope leads to the main palapa with its vast room opening to the swimming pool and sunbathing area, which are staggered to match the shifting levels of the seashore. The principle of "less is more" rules the interior.

CAREYES

At Careyes the mountains descend to
the Pacific as green becomes pink then
the blue of the ocean and turtles lay
their eggs in the sand here twice a year,
giving the place this name that means
"tortoise shell." Careyes merges into
other picturesque landscapes near
Puerto Vallarta, dissolving into a land
where solitude is a gift, where silence is
a norm broken only by the incessant
murmur of the sea as it breaks upon
beach and cliff.

Architecture of the Mexican Pacific
Coast is at its freest here where the new
palapa develops with no pre-determined
limit to its form or height. These vast
spaces resolve the problems of the
body and nourish the soul. The walls
are alive with the vibrant colors of
Mexican fruits.

On the coast of Jalisco, the first "new palapa" built by architect Marco Aldaco was Casa Mi Ojo.

Rising out of rocks pounded by the surf, Casa Mi Ojo is an act of architectural defiance. The architect's first challenge was to show that a palapa could be functional in this milieu. By mistake one day, a local man brought in a tree trunk wound with strangler-fig vines. This error was the beginning of a new style for the columns that would serve as the supports for the palapas of Careyes.

A patio enclosed by a folding-screen-wall and topped by a reed-grass roof open to the play of light and shadow, this is the entrance to architect Diego Villaseñor's creation Casa Talec. The entryway ushers the visitor into the large hall or central palapa, then on to the swimming pool that seems to stretch all the way to the sea, to rooms for the morning and rooms for the afternoon, to a jacuzzi that juts from a black wall over a pebblestone seaweed design in the style of Matisse emerging from the pink ground of a colorwashed wall.

It is hot. Bare feet tread hammered terrazzo floors, carpeted with stones bearing geometric designs.

Playa Rosa and Careyitos are rounded and spangled with palm trees. Also round is the table in the dining room of Casa Torre. The paunchy clay pots from Oaxaca echo the same curving shape. Multiple stairways bridge the various levels that separate the living room from the dining room, and lead to a more intimate space, the pergola, where one goes to watch the sunset. The stairs then spiral onward to another palapa.

Designed by architect Diego Villaseñor, this house rises amid winding paths flanked on either side by ferns.

The quadrangle of the blue tower is clothed in apricot by the low wall that wraps around it. Between the skirting wall and the tower a staircase climbs upward to reveal Teopa Beach, where the green turtle spawns.

The lintels are broken by a wall that folds itself into a screen, then shrinks to become a low wall, then unfolds again and transforms itself into a room divider. It shrinks again, stretches itself, and punctures to form a niche. A window frames a lofty maguey. The edges grow smooth. The angles dissolve.

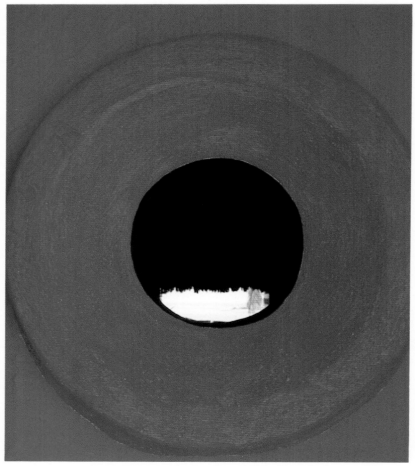

The navel of the sea—Playa Rosa—
pulses with the rhythm of the waves, the
beating of pelican wings, the flavor of an
indigenous architecture and birds fly in
flights of dreams.

Varying shades of purple spread over the colorwashed walls of Casa Encantada, setting off a large clay pot from Michoacán and a stone pillar based on a pre-Hispanic motif. The bignonia is another purple wall dropping its flowers to cover the terrace.

In the main patio, a four-petal pebblestone lotus marks the crux of the house.

In Casa Tigre, designed by the architects Villaseñor and Sánchez, every room has its own time, its own moment, its own silence, its own meditation. Life without doors or windows is one of the architects' great achievements. The main palapa is supported by four lintels made of palm-tree and guayabillo trunks.

There is simplicity in the decor, as in the rustic furniture and the choice of colors. The house is ocher on the outside and white on the inside.

Facing the open sea, Casa los Riscos is faithful to the Spanish concept of water in the patio, here in the shape of a horseshoe, shaded by the long eyelashes of the palapas that surround it and shelter it from both rain and sun.

This is a simple house, with the small-town feel of its baseboards, with doors and windows framed in the same color.

The pelicans have lent their name to this place where the swimming pool seems to blend with the sea, water against water amid coconut groves.

No Mexican beach house is without its hammock. In some of the earliest colonial chronicles, Sahagún spoke of network beds hung in mid-air. He said the natives "used certain network hammocks to move about where they wanted to go."

In 1584, Friar Antonio de Ciudad Real described them thus: "They commonly weave them of locally-grown hemp fabric, although some are of cotton cloth. They are all long and narrow." They came to Mexico from the Caribbean.

In the patio at Casa los Pelícanos, the Michoacán-style hammock invites us to enjoy a siesta.

Casa Tigre del Mar, conceived by its owner and supervised by architect Jean-Claude Galibert, holds sacred the secret language of the *javelinas*, the deer, the crocodiles, the herons, and the wild ducks of the surrounding forest. This house is a plant standing by the sea—a plant that, painted in the titanium shades of the sand, brings out the transparency of the blue and the red—a plant that allows one to live in the heart of its photosynthesis. "One morning," recounts the owner, "I plucked a bougainvillea blossom, a buttercup and a plumbago flower; I took them to the painter and told him: 'Put the colors of these three flowers on the walls.'"

It pleased him to think of building a house from which he could leap into the sea and into the horizon, from the main tower to the highest of the terraces; to descend the rounded steps leading to the half-moon of the swimming pool opening out fan-like; and on the floor, the design motif of the Chartres Cathedral labyrinth, symbol of the Old World's arrival at the Pacific.

107

MANZANILLO

Manzanillo, whose name derives from the manchineel tree that abounds in the state of Colima, was founded in 1522. On either side of the city are two natural bays, between the paired watchtower peaks of Vigía Grande and Vigía Chico, and between the lagoons of Cuyutlán and San Pedrito.

Hernán Cortés launched exploratory expeditions from Manzanillo, and forty-two years later, Miguel López de Legazpi disembarked from the nearby port of Barra de Navidad to conquer the Philippines for the Spanish Crown. López de Legazpi set sail in ships built by Indians and Spaniards on the beaches of Salahua, near the present-day location of the resort at Las Hadas.

When architect Marco Aldaco set out to build this house in Manzanillo, his first move was to seek out vestiges and clues to the proper orientation of the house—to see how the rains fall, to feel the direction of the wind and how it blows.

On site he found the vestiges of a campfire. This is where the caretaker came to eat, where the best breezes blew. Each person's instinct leads him to the one place, the right place.

The entryway is full of mystery and shadows cast by coconut trees, climbing plants, *piñanona* vines and ferns.

Aldaco has elevated the bedrooms to capture the breeze through vertical windows.

The palapa, handwoven by a local artisan, rests on an octagon of columns decorated with indigenous designs.

115

Basing his work on an approach to construction traditional among the Mayans, with their profound knowledge of the stars and their influence on nature, Jalisco architect Manuel Vizcaíno built Casa Villa Paz at San Juan de Lima facing north, putting it in direct contact with the stars. The apertures in the triangular thatched roof protect it from cyclones.

The walls were built according to the pajarilla system, working with a wattle and daub that incorporates mangrove veins in order to allow the material to contract naturally without cracking. The walls are then smoothed to create a surface ready for whitewash or paint. Outside, on the sand, a pathway of split palm tree trunks leads to the bay.

IXTAPA
ZIHUATANEJO

Some 130 miles north of Acapulco,
and only a few minutes drive from the
megaproject of Ixtapa, lies Zihuatanejo—
the "Place of Women." Between one port
and the next there is a series of small
towns ensconced in the Sierra Madre
among beaches, bays and cliffs.

Zihuatanejo is still a traditional seaport
with its dolphins, turtles and pelicans,
where fishermen harvest eel and
a variety of native fishes. The local
microclimate provides cool sea
breezes throughout the day and
mountain breezes at night.

Seashells and snail shells are the
decorative motif. The song of the snail
emerges from the sea and melds into a
new tune, as if Vivaldi were molding the
forms and blending them with the royal
palm, with the straw of the palapas, with
the doors chiseled out of the mass of
red cedar veins, with the Brazil
marshlands timber cut into flakes that fly
about like confetti before settling into a
tropical parquet.

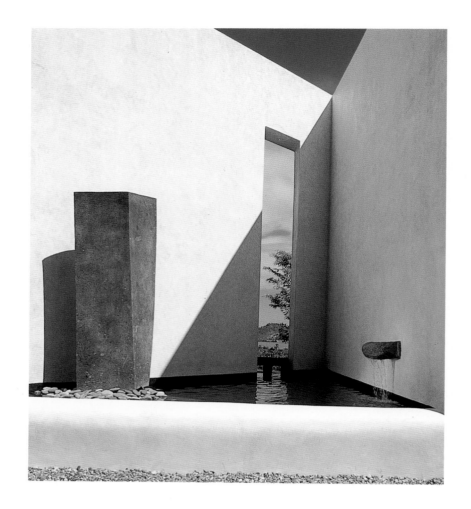

Casa el Cantil, designed by architect Manolo Mestre, rises from the highlands of a peninsula, surrounded by the beaches of Don Rodrigo, Las Cuatas, Playa Triste and Playa Linda. "I wanted to raise the ocean up to the house," says Mestre. "The swimming pool pours out its waters and merges visually with the infinite ocean." In homage to Luis Barragán, the architect playfully placed corner fountains in the patios.

Mestre chose three native cactuses to form the axis of his project, one to mark each level of this split-level house.

He has incorporated certain aspects of Mexico's colonial heritage into the courtyard—archways, fountains, and a Roman impluvium that collects rainwater from the roof and directs it to an underground storage tank.

From the vantage point of a scenic outlook, a meditation site inspired by Chichén Itzá, the island-spangled ocean reminds the observer of a Zen garden.

At Casa Marivent, architect Diego Villaseñor has modified his palapas to introduce the essential element of water, using fountains and canals that evoke the spirit of La Alhambra. Concrete reveals the sensuality of angles where the swimming pool's border meets itself, along the edge of the stairway, and wherever walls meet floors.

From the Petacalco shore north of Zihuatanejo, the builders have gathered rocks striking for their color and shape, rocks that form carpets on the floor and ornament the bases of columns.

130

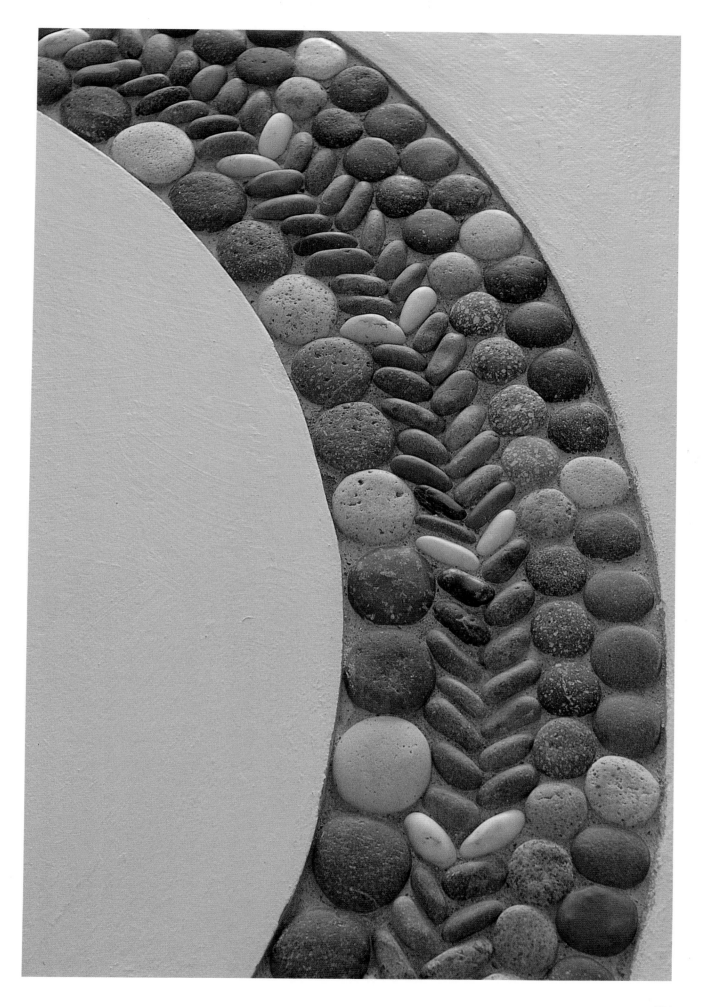

Also designed by architect Diego Villaseñor, Casa el Caracol opens out onto Ixtapa Bay. Spectacular is the word for this swimming pool, whose forms incorporate the wildness of nature in this place.

Next to the pool the great palapa shelters the living room, and behind the wall, on the second level, is the dining area. Freedom and openness are the ruling concepts.

133

In a syndrome reminiscent of Gauguin, Casa la Luna is a hut-like palapa for artists like painters Julian Schnabel and Larry Rivers.

This is a romantic house where the beds are draped with white mosquito nets and the bed covers are hand-woven in Oaxaca. Reeds form the walls and carved wood forms the Michoacán-style columns supporting the tile roof over a small terrace.

137

Influenced by the 16th-century fortresses at San Juan de Ulúa and Campeche, young architects Enrique Zozaya and Enrique Müller have brought their fresh and innovative touch to Playa la Ropa. They have taken high walls and dressed them in vernacular textures.

At La Casa que Canta, the architects work with the concept of a village inn, open and refined. Royal palms, straw, hay, adobe, concrete and tropical hardwoods are the ingredients of this architectural confection.

141

Designer Nicole Dugal juggles a riot of colors and textures at Quinta Troppo, with the help of her friends Zozaya and Müller. The roofs are covered with royal palm, straw or tile. Dugal's feminine touch is felt in the sensuousness of the knotted decor of netting and hammocks. Bare feet traverse shades of blue or aquamarine on the way perhaps to a Mexican-pink niche where a flower vase rules from its shrine.

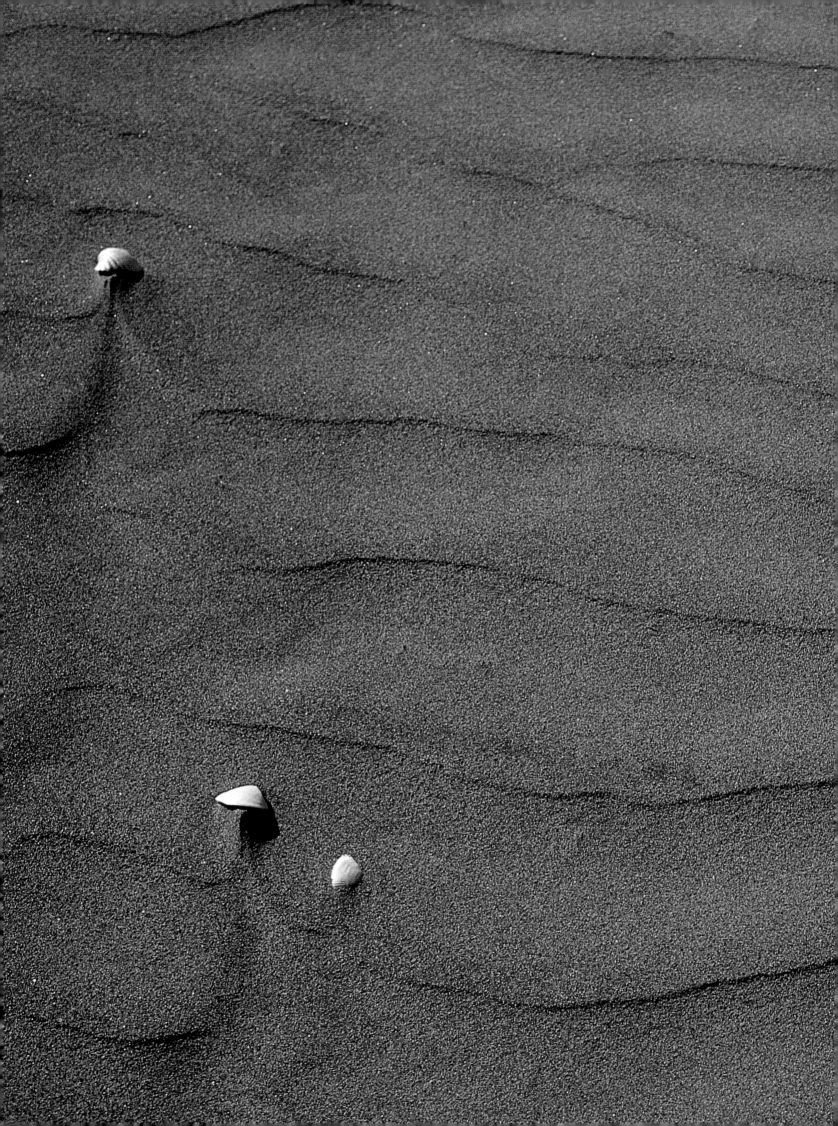

ACAPULCO

Acapulco is a Nahuatl name meaning "Where There Are Thick Canes." It is one of the world's most beautiful bays, with 80°F weather almost all year round.

Acapulco became part of the Aztec empire when it was conquered by King Ahuizotl.

During colonial times the port grew in importance as it launched ships loaded with silver and received the famous Nao de China, the China Fleet, loaded with silk, porcelain and spices en route to Veracruz and thence Europe.

Acapulco is a mosaic of little pieces, each with something special: lizards in Laguna Tres Palos, coconut groves in Puerto Márquez, sharks in Pie de la Cuesta. Acapulco nestles in a warm ocean that spreads over beaches of the finest sand.

Legend has it that one day Gloria Guinness went to El Revolcadero Beach, where she was struck by the simplicity of some hammocks with white mosquito nets gently swaying in the breeze in a wood and bamboo hut. She decided to build a new home radically different from the international style then prevalent in Acapulco. In her nephew Marco Aldaco she discovered the echo of her own dreams, and the complicity to achieve an authentic design.

Acting with a sculptor's sensibility, the architect designed his first palapa for the Guinnesses, its great roof expanding in volume and proportion, thus launching a new style in Mexican architecture.

The setting is serenely laid out amid fragrant mazes, lush foliage and tropical trees that cast their shade on balconies and winding stairwells. This is not just a house; it is a collection of spaces, some of them rendering others invisible.

The Guinnesses and Aldaco traveled in search of the best handicraft in the country. They ordered pieces custom-tailored to the scale of the palapa, big urns from Puebla and pottery from Michoacán. They visited Gorky's Guanajuato and worked with craftsmen and artists, sharing a sophisticated informality with them.

Enormous *petates*, or straw rugs, were woven; Martha Aldaco's brush carpeted the exterior cement staircases and covered the floors with geometric patterns.

Native designs decorate the window trimming, headboards and stucco columns, with puffed cushions covered in Oaxacan huipiles resting against them. This carefully crafted mosaic achieves an ensemble unlike anything ever seen before.

154

Next to the sea stands Casa los Helechos, the second architectural work by Marco Aldaco in Acapulco, where his intuition was given free reign.

From under the fringed palapa unfolds a panorama of Acapulco's spectacular bay.

This house is a stage set for pleasure; one of its spectacles is the party to celebrate the New Year. Candles light the path; plants flutter. Tropical music approaches; guitar trios emerge. Suddenly a foghorn interrupts, but then a mariachi trumpet blares into being a cornucopia of exotic fruits, lobster, ceviche and shrimp.

Amid palm trees and boulders rises the double-pitched palapa of Casa Mabruk, meaning "Be Thou Blessed" in Arabic. From Mabruk, the view of the stars; from Mabruk, a game of paddle tennis; from Mabruk, a sense of protection. Architecture is neither a whim of shape nor is it art for art's sake. It did not go unnoticed when the caretaker built a small palm-leaf roof between two rocks, where the breeze was best, where animals passed in search of the shortest path. The steep, rocky terrain was a special challenge for architect Marco Aldaco, which he met by listening to the ancient wisdom of the coast, the intuition of the indigenous people.

"Aldaco drew some very amusing plans; he put sandals at the foot of the bed, a knife in the kitchen and a fish in the pool. His plans are not very conventional," says the owner. "That's why we liked them."

The house is built on three different levels and is wrapped in a certain mystery. Upstairs are the bedrooms, in the middle the palapa, and down below is the swimming pool, with its high yellow wall designed to conserve heat and reflect it into the water.

164

Ceramic cats, seals, squirrels and donkeys have taken over the pool area. In the rest of the house there are chairs from Michoacán, flower pots from Tlaquepaque, majolica from Guanajuato, Puebla tile, hand-embroidered cushions from Guerrero, and blown glass from the state of Mexico.

PUNTA ZICATELA

The coast of Oaxaca at Punta Zicatela is defined by its plains, by its winds, by the lagoons that reflect its migrating flocks of pink storks, gray herons, pelicans, ospreys, bluejays and hawks.

Between the Sierra Madre Oriental and the Sierra Madre Occidental lies the Nudo Mixteco, the Mixtecan Knot where sixteen ethnic groups intersect as they sketch out their different languages and create a mosaic of costumes in counterpoint to the local environment.

The long skirts of the Tehuanas float in the wind in this climate with its 78°F climate. The hands of the Juchiteca women skilfully twine their hair, weaving art into their braids as the Mixteca and Zapotec women do, forever recreating the pattern, for here there is no craft but that of Oaxaca.

Oaxaca, seated in her wooden chair, wrapped in her *petates*, climbs up the mountain range and back down to the city, creating fancies as she goes, then returns to Zicatela, to the houses conceived by architect Diego Villaseñor, where color tones defy rationality and reshape space, compressing or stretching distances at their whim, where some things are hidden away only to highlight others.

A certain attitude toward this place is important to be in harmony with Punta Zicatela, where every stone, every tree and every window has a worth of its own.

More than just seaside architecture, the 24 houses built to a common plan by Diego Villaseñor develop a whole new concept—a way of life based on peace, quiet and respect for privacy.

This ecological community combines constructed and natural spaces, where the architect has framed circles with stonework borders and taken care to keep the shifting levels of the floor unobtrusive. The design of the walls stands in unique relationship to the floors and ceilings.

At Punta Zicatela, the house-dweller learns to live in drought and rainfall, with leafy trees or bare ones. Within this context, everything has meaning. The palapas are tightly woven. Like a Toledo painting, white crab shells cover a comal, while bean pods cross paths on another. Margarita Alvarez directs the overall craft design.

189

As simply as a growing vine, this
architecture surrenders itself to the sun,
to the coast of Oaxaca, to the ecology
of this place. The floor catches striped
shadows, moving shadows, shadows
now clawing, now caressing, now
embracing—they are purple columns,
palm leaves fringing palapas, roundness
of stones, of pots, of urns that stand at
the foot of a wall, of women who lose
themselves in hammocks while rocking
as shadows fill silhouettes, coming and
going like the sea until the sunset lulls
them to sleep.

In the grandeur of this landscape there
is a movie script to be read, a life to be
enacted, thought sensations to be lived,
spaces and times to be mapped. One
becomes aware of space, of a space
and time holding the time that lies
within us.

HUATULCO

Huatulco, which means "Place Where the Tree is Worshiped," derives its name from an ancient legend. They say that when the Spaniards arrived at this amazing series of bays in the 16th century, they found that the Indians were worshiping an enormous, indestructible cross that had been standing in this place for several centuries.

Architect Ricardo Legorreta's presence is strong in Huatulco. When he arrived at Tangolunda Bay for the first time, by boat, he visualized, from the architect's point of view, a house sheltered in the strength of the sea.

In a conversation about a home that Legorreta was building in Bosques de las Lomas in Mexico City, Luis Barragán said: "How brave of you, Ricardo, to build a house with a two-pitched roof!" Also double-pitched was the roof on the blue house Legorreta later built in Huatulco. With its ocean-blue walls, the house sways in time with the beat of the waves.

"There is a potent relationship between the way you design a space and they way you live in it," says Legorreta. "Architecture is worthless unless it is related to the site."

This is not just a guest-house; it has its own soul. It blends its own perfume made of the aromas of banana and honeysuckle, night-blooming jasmine and lime, because this is an architecture of fragrances as well.

At Zaashila, architect Javier Sordo gave flight to his imagination and conceived a truly daring swimming pool design. Submerged cots and tables built into the side of the pool permit guests to sunbathe while refreshing themselves in the cool water at the same time. The pool is of poured white concrete. Because it is uncoated and unpainted, it is uniquely transparent.

Mediterranean in their inspiration, Zaashila's windows are freely designed. The architect strove to create dreams and fantasies in this hotel built like a residential inn.

A frame built of tropical wood forms a composition with two semi-circular windows and holds a series of shelves where potted plants rest. Round wooden beams shade the steps of a staircase. The combination of stucco and wood enhances the contrast of the lighting and gives warmth.

"If I were not an architect, I would be a movie director," says Santiago Aspe. And he is right. The romanticism of the bath, of the master bedroom, of the central swimming pool and the gazebo of Casa Yoocaabee, all illustrate Aspe's imagistic calling.

Before beginning the project, Aspe lived and traveled extensively with his clients, just as Frank Lloyd-Wright used to do. Communication between the architect and the homeowners is indispensable if practical needs and dreams are to be harmonized.

Aspe first examined the terrain, drew its topography and allowed the local ecosystem to enter into his life. He incorporated the house into its natural environment; this is not a house in the middle of a garden but a house on a hill.

La Picuda, designed by Carlos Herrera

in Huatulco, is a never-ending solstice.

The sun pours into the space and its

niches smile with colors vibrating in

ocher, indigo, and ocean-blue angles.

The niches look out on the sea, open to

its response—a wave, another wave, an

ocean perennially alive, always awake,

deep, mysterious, voluptuous,

ceaselessly wallowing in its own foam,

eager to surrender it.

Following the general trend of modern Mexican architecture in its approach to walls, textures, and colors, Herrera looks for new ways to apply traditional materials using inviting angles.

He has carved geometric shapes out of huge walls to let the sea in, to allow it to have impact. Whatever the mood of the sea, be it weakness, strength, or self-absorption, the house is penetrated by its odor and strength, impregnated with its sound . . . The sea undulates on its way to the patio with its Pharaonic proportions. This patio is the essence of the architectural concept, and takes its triangular shape, which is the basis of the design, from the shape of the land.

Also triangular is the rock fountain in a corner, as are the noon shadows. The abstractness of the courtyard puts the mind in a mood to feel the impact of the seascape, where the island of Montosa lies framed by a broad open space in the living room. The patio, filled with sand, reminds us of the desert.

On the Pacific Coast, Mexico sings a
song of a vernacular and contemporary
architecture—where the sea is a
childhood memory that calls forth the
passing of a whale, the flight of a
pelican, a fisherman's boat, a dream of
this seaside architecture where the
palapa drenched in saltwater fills up
with sand, plays with its own freedom
and shares it.

217

1 LOS CABOS
2 PUERTO VALLARTA
3 CAREYES
4 MANZANILLO
5 IXTAPA ZIHUATANEJO
6 ACAPULCO
7 PUNTA ZICATELA
8 HUATULCO

140–141 Grass roofs and the texture of straw on the walls of Casa que Canta, which launched a new architectural style in Zihuatanejo.

146 This stepped adobe wall divides the living room from the bedroom. In the background, the interior of the palapa.

147 A canvas cot rests on a blue concrete floor.

ACAPULCO

150–151 Panoramic view of the palapa at sunset. Wide stairsteps fan out toward the bay. Multicolored pebblestone forms geometric patterns in the hammered terrazzo floor.

152 View of the living room under the round palapa. In the niches, handicrafts from Jalisco and Oaxaca.

153 On the dining table, a Oaxacan tablecloth, bougainvilleas from the garden and Pueblo chairs. Also Pueblo in style is the blue baseboard that runs along the walls and around the door frames. Over the polished terrazzo floor, a petate specially woven for this room. A colonial archangel sits in a niche.

158 Detail of the Jalisco-style painted concrete floor by Martha de Aldaco, with flowers and geometric patterns based on Tonalá designs.

159 A Santa María shawl draped over the backrest of a rattan armchair.

162 On the open terrace of a bungalow, chairs from Michoacán. A colonial sunburst made of wood adorns the wall.

163 The dining room, with some of the immense ferns that have given this house its name. Beautiful collection of majolica from Puebla amid columns painted by architect Marco Aldaco.

164 The exterior of the bedroom area of Casa Mabruk.

Detail of a ceramic tub from Tonalá filled with seashells and snail shells.

165 "Better the grace of imperfection than graceless perfection," as architect Alex von Wuthenau once said. The concept applies to this irregularly stepped terrace and the paint that frames the light incorporated into the wall. Chair from Michoacán.

166–167 Grounds of the residential area at Casa Mabruk.

168 The palapa structure is intriguing. When cut in optimal conditions under a new moon, the roof cover can last up to 15 years.

169 Tonalá pottery, Gorky majolica and china jars from Puebla enliven the dining area.

170–171 This spectacular swimming pool, designed by architect Ignacio Rodríguez for Casa de la Playa, is like the sacred cenote, or sinkhole, of Yucatán where offerings and sacrifices were made. The pool is surrounded by sculpted rocks.